IPHONE 12 PRO USER GUIDE

The Complete Beginner And Seniors Guide On How To Use The New iPhone 12 Pro(2020) With Advanced Tips And Trick To Help You Master IPhone 12 Pro.

By

Kelvin L. Wilson

Table of Contents

INTRODUCTION

Adjust the color and hue if necessary.

A male portrait taken with a wide camera on the iPhone 12 Pro.

The new seven-element wide camera makes bright pictures and videos even in low light.

Male portrait photographed in black and white using an iPhone 12 Pro projection camera.

The TV cameras on the iPhone 12 Pro and iPhone 12 ProMax are perfect for classic framed portraits, for closer shots and narrower cultures.

In front

Night mode enhancements, now extended to TrueDepth and Ultra Wide cameras, allow for a brighter image. And night time mode provides longer exposure times for sharper videos, better lighting paths and smoother exposure in low light scenarios used with a tripod. Deep Fusion, now better and faster, comes to all cameras, and with the new smart HDR 3, users can watch more accurate images, even in complex scenes.

The iPhone 12 Pro models offer the highest quality video on the smartphone, and are the only cameras and devices in the world that allow an end-to-end experience for HDR video with Dolby Vision, up to 60 frames per second, and even better video stabilization for film class productions. Dolby Vision takes advantage of the Super Retina XDR display for stunning contrast when shooting and listening to video, and users can share Their videos with AirPlay support up to 4K Dolby Vision on external devices.

for HDR video with Dolby Vision. A film shot in an HDR video with Dolby Vision on the iPhone 12 Pro, by photographer Emanuel "Chibo" Lubzki.

Realistic AR and innovative camera experiences

An all-new LiDAR scanner comes with the Pro Line, which offers the option to measure light distance and use scene pixel depth information. This technology delivers faster and more realistic AR experiences and improves autofocus 6 times in low light for greater accuracy and reduced shooting time in photos and videos. This advanced hardware, combined with the power of the A14 Bionic's neural motor, also releases portraits from night mode, giving a beautiful bokeh effect with low light.

Night mode portrait, powered by a LiDAR scanner, was taken on an iPhone 12 Pro.

New and innovative accessories with MagSafe

MagSafe enhances wireless charging for a better and more efficient experience and brings an ecosystem of easy-to-connect accessories to complement iPhone 12 Pro models beautifully. 7 MagSafe provides a unique iPhone experience, with a set of magnets around the wireless charging coil, adapted for alignment and efficiency, that connects perfectly to the iPhone every time. MagSafe chargers efficiently provide up to 15W of power, but Qi-capable devices still exist. Charging solutions include the MagSafe charger and the MagSafe Duo charger for iPhone and Apple Watch use, as well as new silicone cases, leather and clear, simply clinging to the back of the iPhone and a leather sports wallet. Customers can also view innovative MagSafe accessories from third-party manufacturers.

MagSafe charging stations on iPhone 12 Pro.

MagSafe accessories for iPhone 12 Pro.

GIF demonstrating the easy and secure connection of a MagSafe charger to the iPhone 12 Pro.

The new and innovative MagSafe system enables smooth and powerful wireless charging and convenient accessories for construction.

GIF file demonstrating the easy connection of MagSafe accessories to iPhone 12 Pro.

The new and innovative MagSafe system enables smooth and powerful wireless charging and convenient accessories for construction.

iOS 14

iOS 14 provides a re-iPhone experience with new ways to customize the home screen. Beautifully designed widgets display information at a glance and can be set to different sizes on any home screen page.

iOS 14 also brings new ways to discover and use apps with App Clips, powerful updates to stay in touch with Messages, greener ways to discover cities with enhanced Maps and privacy features for even more transparency and control.

CHAPTER ONE

SETUP IPHONE 12 PRO

Mazel Tov! You are now the proud owner of a new iPhone 12 or iPhone 12 Pro. You probably want to dive straight into the phone as soon as you get the box in your hands, but try to contain your excitement and prepare a little!

We have small installation tips you will want to pay attention to.

Show me

- Backup and restore

You can back up using iCloud, iTunes or Finder.

For Mac Backup (macOS Catalina): Connect your old iPhone to your Mac, open a new Finder window and select your iPhone in the left column in the Locations section. You will see a window that looks like the iPhone administration window that was previously in iTunes. In the Select Backups section, back up all the data on your iPhone to this Mac. Encrypting a local backup is a good idea, so back up your account password and health data as well - choose a password you won't forget. Click the button to make a backup now.

Macos Catalina iPhone Finder

In macOS Catalina you can access your iPhone using Finder.

For Mac Backup (MacOS Mojave and later): The backup process is similar to the one described above for Catalina, but instead you use the iTunes app. After backing up your old iPhone, plug in your new one. iTunes takes you through the setup steps.

When you set up your new iPhone 12, you can recover your iPhone from this backup after connecting with your Apple ID on your new device.

If you happen to come from an Android phone (hey, welcome to kindergarten!), There is an Android Move app on iOS that can help you get all your Google account data and mail, calendars and contacts, your camera flips over, even your Chrome bookmarks are transferred On safari.

Quick start

You will go through the rest of the installation process when you turn on Face ID and then your phone will be ready to use, set up like your old iPhone. It will also ask you to update your old iPhone's backup satellite if it does not wear out a bit.

Setting up your phone this way conveys most of your settings, your home screen arrangement and more. It saves a huge amount of time. But it does require iOS 11 or later, so if for some reason you are absent for years without updating your iPhone at least to iOS 11 (or the current version, iOS 14) for some reason, you should upgrade immediately. You do not want to wait for a major update process when you have your iPhone 12 in hand.

Once you have finished your phone this way, you will want to take some time to download all your apps. Initially your phone displays placeholders for your apps, everything is neat and full of folders just like on your old iPhone. But your new phone needs to download apps, because every time you download an app from the app store, your phone actually grabs a unique version specifically tailored to this iPhone model. But your user data and settings are transferred, which is the important part.

As fast and easy as possible, we recommend that you back up your phone as described in number 1 above. If something really goes wrong with your installation process, you'll be glad you did!

- Set up Face ID

Setting up Face ID is also much faster than Touch ID - the installation screen to which I invite you and ask you to look around a few times.

Apple Face ID Setup

Face ID setup is much faster than Touch ID.

Worried about your privacy using Face ID? Not to be. No pictures of your face and no other biometric data will leave your phone - Apple will get nothing from it. And it is not accessible by other applications, as other applications have not been able to access your fingerprint using a touch ID. You can read all about it in our FAQ about Face ID.

Since you need to allow Face ID to use Apple Pay, this would be a good time to hop to the Apple Wallet app to set it up. If you're new to Apple Pay, just follow the instructions in your wallet to add a credit card or two. Your wallet history will still be there, but you will need to enter new payment cards that you want to use with Apple Pay. (For information nAnd more about Apple Pay, see our full guide.)

- Update whether apps

Great, now you should be on your home screen on your new iPhone, finally. Open the App Store first - you want the latest versions of all your apps. To check for app updates, launch the App Store app and click on your account icon in the top right corner. You will find an update section below all your account information and you can get the updates here. If you use fast installation, most of your apps already need to be updated, so this is fast, fast.

Keep in mind that you can update your apps automatically by turning on the update switch in Settings> App Store> App Updates. Alternatively, you can update your apps manually and simply check the "What's New" release notes to see what has changed.

- Adjust your Apple Watch

If you're using an Apple Watch (or you may have just bought a new Apple Watch to take care of your new phone) you need to pair it with your new iPhone to keep your activity data and health running and your new phone alerts updated. Flows to your watch. First you need to disconnect your watch from your old iPhone, in the Apple Watch app on your old iPhone (tap your watch, then the "i" icon, then click on Apple Watch and enter your iCloud password when prompted. Is), or on the watch itself settings > General> Reset).

If your Apple Watch is still not running watchOS 7, you may want to update it. To upgrade, your Apple Watch must be connected to its charger, within range of your iPhone, and must be at least 50 percent charged. Then check if there is a software update option in the iPhone Watch app.

LEARN THE NEW GESTURES AND COMMANDS

As you may have noticed, your iPhone 12 does not have a home button. Where there was a home button, now you have another half inch of fancy OLED!

If you come from an iPhone X, XS or 11, it will of course be very familiar. But if you are upgrading from an older iPhone or iPhone SE, you need to learn some new gestures.

Here are some basic commands you should learn now when your iPhone is "free at home".

Back to home: Just scroll down from the bottom of the screen. easy!

Jump between apps: Swipe left or right along the bottom edge of the phone to skip between apps. You can sort "flip" from the bottom corners, move your finger up and down, "jump" between apps, or just slide directly side by side along the bottom edge.

App Switcher: Slide up from the bottom edge and pause for a moment with your finger still on display. App cards pop up quickly, and you can lift your finger and slide around.

Close App: If you need to kill an app from the app switch, just click up.

There are many more new commands and gestures to learn. You are in luck: we have a guide for that!

- Upload it, fast!

There's a reason your new iPhone 12 holds that shiny glass, and it's not because it's a fall for the iPhone 4. No, because the glass is back to support wireless charging. To use this feature, you need a compatible charging pad that uses the Qi standard (we tested a bunch, and here are some of our favorites). If you have one of those lying down, simply put your iPhone on the surface and see how it starts to open. Say goodbye to the noise of lightning cables on the bedside table!

With the iPhone 12, Apple introduced a new feature called MagSafe. This is a new magnetically installed charger similar to other Qi wireless chargers, only with secure magnetic alignment. Precise alignment and new internal circuits allow Apple to increase charging speeds by up to 15 watts - twice as fast as regular Qi plantations and almost a lightning cable.

CHARGING WIRES FOR IPHONE

Of course, you can charge your iPhone 12 using Lightning if you want. In fact, it is always the fastest way to charge your phone if you use the appropriate power adapter and cable. The iPhone 12 supports fast charging in the USB-C Power Delivery (USB-PD) standard. Anything over 15 watts will charge your iPhone pretty quickly.

> ➢ Prepare your memos

Memoji are cool, but Memoji takes them to the next level. If you upgraded from iPhone X or iPhone 11, you may have already created memoji. If iPhone 12 is your first iPhone with a TrueDepth front camera system, this is your first chance to build your cartoon avatar.

If iPhone 12 is your first TrueDepth-enabled iPhone, it's time to make your memo!

Start opening the messaging app and then open a new message or existing thread. Tap the Animoji icon at the bottom and then the + sign at the top of the Animoji list.

We have a step-by-step memoji guide that will guide you through the process.

 ➢ Set up your medical ID

- Setting up a medical iPhone

You can get information about your medical ID from the keypad.

We have compiled for you a quick and easy guide to defining the details of your medical ID that can be accessed from the emergency wipers even when your phone is locked.

- See Apple User Guide

Did you know that Apple has a very detailed user guide (hundreds of pages!) That tells you everything you need to know about your iPhone 12 hardware and the latest version of iOS?

The iPhone user guide is a great web resource, but you can also download it for free in the books app.

You can access the iPhone user guide online, search or search for what you want to know. This is a good bookmarking site. Instead you can download the iBook version for free in the books app. if youE Need help, you may not be in a place where you have easy internet access.

CHAPTER TWO

USE EMERGENCY SOS ON YOUR IPHONE

When you call using SOS, your iPhone automatically dials the local emergency number.. For example, in mainland China you can choose police, fire or ambulance.

You can also attach emergency contacts. After an emergency call, your iPhone alerts emergency contacts via SMS unless you choose to cancel.

CALL EMERGENCY SERVICES

hold the side buttons and the volume buttons until the emergency SOS indicator appears.

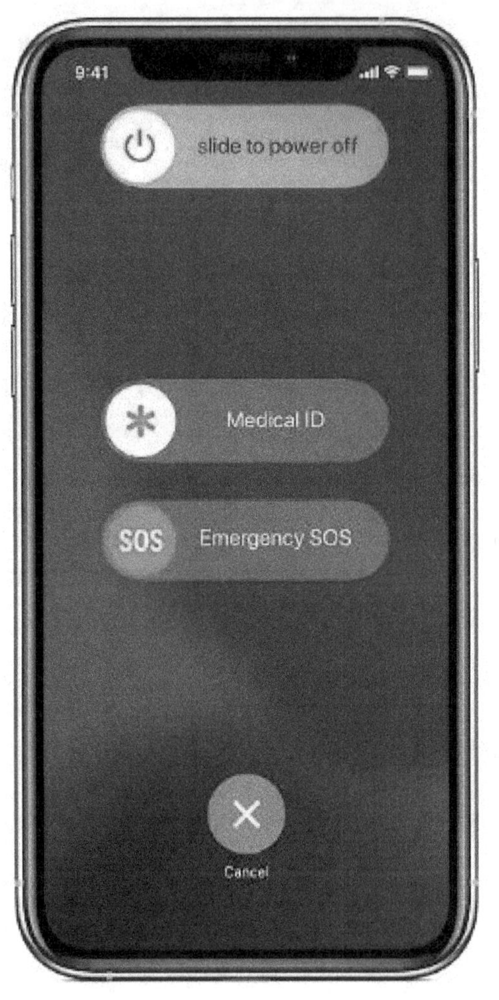

Drag the Emergency SOS slider to call the emergency services. If you keep pressing the side and volume buttons instead of pulling the slider, a countdown will start and an alarm will sound. If you hold down the button until the countdown is complete, your iPhone automatically calls the emergency services.

STOP SHARING YOUR LOCATION

When your location is shared, you will receive a reminder to stop every 4 hours for 24 hours.

If you start counting down by accident, you can cancel. On iPhone 8 or later, release the side button and the volume down button. On iPhone 7 or later, click the Stop button and then click Stop Call.

If you make an emergency call, you can stop the call. Tap the red end call icon, then confirm that you want to call.

REMOVE EMERGENCY CONTACTS

- .
- Turn Open the health app and tap on your profile picture.
- Tap for medical identification.
- Tap Edit, and tap on Emergency Contacts.
- Tap the Delete button next to a contact, then click Delete.
- Tap Done to save your changes

OFF THE AUTOMATIC CALL

When automatic calling is active and you are trying to make an emergency call, your iPhone triggers a countdown and sounds an alarm. Once the countdown is complete, your iPhone will automatically call the emergency services.

Here's how to change the setting:

- Lunched the Settings app.
- Press SOS for emergency.
- Turn the automatic call on or off.

- If this setting is turned off, you can still use the emergency SOS slider to call.

CHANGE THE WAY YOU COMMUNICATE

Here's how to change the setting:

- Go to Settings.
- Press SOS for emergency.
- Call with the side button on or off. Prolonged pressing of the side button along with the volume button will continue to work with its activation.

CHAPTER THREE

HOW TO CONTROL THE CAMERA APP ON IPHONE 12 AND IPHONE 12 PRO

The camera app on the iPhone 12 and iPhone 12 Pro has been updated to take advantage of Apple's latest features like night mode portraits and Dolby Vision HDR recording. This way you can make the most of what the camera app has to offer.

The cameras and camera app in the iPhone 12 range are full of features - most of which Apple will not tell you about. For simplicity, and for the camera to "just work", Apple insists that the most common features are the first you will find.

Above them, however, there are different features and different ways to use them. They are all designed to make the images more convenient, powerful - and much faster.

VOLUME BUTTONS

This quick tip, for example, is widely used by many, but some are not yet familiar with this useful trick. Apple allows users to use the volume up and down buttons as physical shutter buttons in the camera app. When the camera app is open, press any button and you type the scroll bar and take a picture.

Moreover, if you press one of the two buttons instead, a video starts. As long as you hold the button, the video will be recorded.

Hold down the volume, however, to shoot fast video

If this is not something you ever want, you can change it. Go to the settings app and set the volume up button to take burst photos instead. Turn it on and now when the volume up button is held, photos explode until you release it.

More QuickTake options

This ability to hold the volume down button to shoot video is a change from what Apple calls QuickTake. In general, QuickTake is a quick way to take a single photo, video, or group of prostituted photos.

From the camera app, tap the white aperture button once to take a picture. Press and hold the button, and now you start recording video without stopping what you are doing and switch to video mode.

When you do, this center button will change from white to red. As soon as you release the aperture button, the video stops recording.

Take bursting images using QuickTake

This is great for very fast videos, but not practical when shooting extended scenes. If you want to keep recording video and do not want to hold the shutter button with your finger all the time, you can hold it in place and then slide it to the right. It locks it in video mode, and you can lower your finger from the glass.

Alternatively, when you tap and slide right and left, burst mode starts shooting until you let go.

You need to get used to how to activate these two different features. However, they present a much faster method of taking these shots without going through all the situations first.

Height-width ratio

It is easy to change the aspect ratio in which you are shooting. Tap the death icon at the top of the camera app and the toolbar will appear above the aperture. Look at the aspect ratio that corresponds to what you are currently shooting for the other selection.

Apple allows you to shoot in squares 4: 3, 16: 9 and 1: 1.

Photography Photography 16: 9

What is very convenient is that if you take a picture in 16: 9 and later decide that you do not want the widescreen format, you can cut it to 4: 3 from the Photos app and it will do so without losing the quality.

SCOPE ADJUSTMENT

The iPhone 12 and iPhone 12 Mini have two cameras - the extra wide lens and the wide lens. From the camera app you can expand to .5X using the extra-wide lens or you can zoom in from 1X to 5X digital zoom.

Just click the 1X icon to quickly jump from 1X to 5X and back. You can also move your finger left and right and slide to pick up a wheel with a sharper zoom level.

The iPhone 12 is limited to 5X digital zoom

The iPhone 12 Pro and the iPhone 12 Pro Max are different. This is because they offer three cameras in place - the extra wide lenses, the widening and the telephoto.

Instead of just a zoom level indicator, the camera app displays 5X, 1X and 2X options - and one chooses to place the iPhone between the three cameras. Also these you can slide to switch from .5X to 10X digital zoom.

When you have finished adjusting the circumference, press the wheel to hide it and return to the quick button.

PORTRAIT MODE

Portrait mode has been around for a while and Apple has continued to improve. Over the years we got different zoom levels, we got the ability in the front camera, we got different L effects of light, and we have the ability to adjust the aperture according to the fact.

For the iPhone 12, there's not much really new stuff here. However, it is now possible to take pictures in portrait mode with different degrees of Boca in the background.

Cover the lens to trick the phone into activating night-time portraits

For comparison, however, this is a great new feature for the iPhone 12 Pro and iPhone 12 Pro Max. It is now possible to take pictures in low light portrait mode, thanks in part to the LiDAR scanner. LiDAR allows the camera to focus quickly and without light.

Night portraits can only be taken at 1X level and if you are trying to shoot at low light at 2X, the icon in the lower right corner tells you to switch to 1X. When night mode is turned on, you will see the night mode icon in the upper right corner.

NIGHT MODE

Speaking of night mode, it is now turned on in all lenses. Night mode can be used with the selfie camera as well as an extra-wide, wide-angle camera and camcorder.

Night mode allows automatic when the light is on, but can also be turned on or off manually. You can see it in the toolbar when we get to the above dimension ratio. It usually chooses the right exposure speed for you, but you can also adjust the slider directly over the aperture faster or slower. These numbers vary depending on how much your phone moves.

When you place the phone on a tripod,Night mode works at an exposure speed of up to 30 seconds for some super bright flashes.

New this year for the iPhone 12 and iPhone 12 Pro is the ability to capture night mode times. These are also activated automatically when the light is low and a timeline begins.

DOLBY VISION

For videographers, the ability to shoot in Dolby Vision HDR right now is a big deal. This is the first mobile phone to capture, edit and share Dolby Vision content.

Although it is a massive luxury feature, it is very easy to use. It only comes down to switching to settings.

To switch to Dolby Vision recording:

- Go to the settings app
- Go to camera
- Then dive into the recording video
- Go to HDR Video

Now that you are shooting video, it is recorded on Dolby Vision HDR.

Dolby Vision HDR Video

After shooting Dolby Vision HDR video, you will find the HDR slider in the upper right corner of the thumbnail in the Photos app. An HDR video also starts at normal brightness but quickly becomes very bright when viewed in the Photos app.

LAST NOTES AND SMALL FEATURES

Apple has been debating its Smart HDR 3 update with these new phones and part of it is a new scene detection mode that helps different images based on what is in the image. For example, it can reveal a better portrait, or adjust the color and contrast in the photo of the food, or increase the saturation in the landscape photo.

HDR will still be used no matter what, but you can disable scene detection in camera settings if you prefer.

Camera app for iPhone 12 and iPhone 12 Pro

Next, Deep Fusion is the magic of Apple's computational photography and previously only worked on the wide lens. Now it also works on extra wide cameras and selfies. Any images with these will look better automatically without any user interaction.

Apple ProRAW is a new image format that will be released on iPhone 12 Pro and iPhone 12 Pro Max in the coming months through a software update.

iPhone 12 Pro camera

Earlier phones, in the iPhone 12, asked users to choose between using Deep Fusion and HDR or shooting in

RAW. Now users do not have to. It uses Deep Fusion and HDR but retains these additional details for editing.

No matter what type of photo you are dealing with, Apple attaches great importance to the camera app and does its best to ensure that you always get the best photos possible.

FULL IPHONE 12 DEVICE

It's hard to argue with Apple's logic that a new user would be inundated with the plethora of options available to them, especially around the camera.

While each user prefers a different set of controls and features more clearly

CHAPTER FOUR

HOW TO SET UP APPLE PAY CASH

First the first thing you need to set up is Apple Pay Cash.

- Open settings.
- Tap Wallet and Apple Pay.
- Tap Apple Pay Cash.
- Tap Continue.

Ask for consent if asked to do so. If you have previously installed Apple Cash on other devices connected to your iCloud account, you may not be prompted to agree

- Tap Done.

VERIFY YOUR IDENTITY FOR APPLE PAY

- Open the settings on your iPhone.
- Tap Wallet and Apple Pay.
- Tap Apple Pay Cash.
- Tap Verified ID.
- Tap Continue.
- Give your first and last name.
- Tap Next.
- Enter your address.
- Tap Next.

HOW TO PUT MONEY IN YOUR APPLE PAY CASH CARD

- Open your iPhone wallet.
- Tap your Apple Pay cash card.
- Tap ... in the black circle in the upper right corner.
- Tap Add money.

Enter the amount of money you would like to add to your card, using the predefined buttons or by entering a custom amount in the number pad.

SEND APPLE PAY CASH TO YOUR BANK ACCOUNT

- Open your iPhone wallet.
- Tap your Apple Pay cash card.
- Tap ... in the black circle in the upper right corner.
- Transfer money to the bank, show how to open the wallet, type Apple Pay Cash Card and click ...
- Tap Transfer to Bank.
- Enter the amount you would like to transfer from your Apple Pay cash balance to your bank account.
- Tap Next.

Choose between direct transfer and 1-3 business days. Please note that direct transfer is taxable and requires a bank card, when choosing 1-3 business days you will need to attach your bank account details.

- Confirm the transfer.

HOW DO I SEND PAYMENTS USING APPLE PAY CASH

Sending money to friends and family in messages is strangely similar to sending a sticker.

- Open messages app
- Tap a conversation with the person you want to send money to or start a new iMessage conversation.
- Click on the Apple Pay button.
- Press the - or + buttons to select an amount.
- Tap Show keyboard if you want to enter a specific amount.
- Enter your specific amount.
- Tap Pay.
- Press the Submit button (looks like an arrow in a black circle).

CLAIM PAYMENT USING APPLE PAY CASH

Of course you can also request payment via messages.

- Open messages on your iPhone.
- Tap a conversation with the person you want to ask for money or start a new iMessage conversation.
- Click on the Apple Pay.
- Press the - or + buttons to select an amount.
- Tap Show keyboard if you want to enter a specific amount.
- Enter your specific amount.
- Tap Request
- Press the Submit button (looks like an arrow in a black circle).

CHAPTER FIVE

DARK MODE

TURN ON DARK MODE

Use night mode on your iPhone

With supported iPhone models, you can use night mode to take pictures when the camera detects an environment in low light.

Take low-light photos with night mode

Night mode will turn on automatically when the camera detects a dim lighting environment. Depending on how dark the scene is, your iPhone may quickly shoot in night mode, or it may take a few seconds. You can also adjust your lighting setting.

For best results, hold the iPhone steady until your finger closes. To pause a night mode image where the photo is completed, simply press the stop button below the slider.

ADJUSTS THE CAPTURE TIME

When shooting in night mode, a number appears next to the night mode icon to indicate how long the shooting lasts.

Then use the slider above the aperture button to select the maximum, which extends the capture time. When you take the picture, Slate sets a timer that will count until the end of the shooting time.

TAKE SELFIES IN NIGHT MODE

- Open the Camera app.

- Press the front camera button.

- Raise and hold your iPhone in your front.

- Take your selfie.

CAPTURE NIGHT TIME VIDEOS

In low light conditions, the night time mode with a tripod can be used to record videos with longer frame rates. Open the camera app and swipe to the left until you see the elapsed time. Tap the Aperture button to shoot your video.

USES A PORTRAIT IN NIGHT MODE

- Open the camera app and slide to portrait mode.

- Follow the on-screen tips.

- Press the aperture button

CHAPTER SIX

SIRI

HOW TO SETUP SIRI

Before taking advantage of the new features released in Siri in iOS 14, you must first verify that Siri is enabled on your iPhone 12.

- Open system.
- Choose Siri & Search.

On the Siri and Search page, make sure the following three options are enabled:

- ☐ Hear "Hey Siri": This allows you to say the wake-up phrase "Hey Siri" to begin interacting with your voice assistant.
- ☐ Press Side Button for Siri - This allows you to wake up Siri by long pressing the button on the right side of the phone.
- ☐ Enable Siri when locked: This allows you to use Siri without unlocking your phone.

HOW TO USE SIRI ON IPHONE 12

Once Siri is enabled on your iPhone 12 to access it, all you have to do is say "Hey Siri" or press and hold the button on the right side of the phone.

With the Siri update in iOS 14, the voice assistant no longer occupies the full screen. Then when you reply, the replies will appear as widgets and banners on one part of your phone screen, but they won't fill the entire screen yet.

CHAPTER SEVEN

HOW TO CHANGE IPHONE 12 MINI LANGUAGE

- ☐ Go to setting

- ☐ Second, open the general part.

- ☐ Then go to the Language and Region tab.

- ☐ Then select the iPhone language and select the preferred language

- When selected, press DONE to change the APPLE iPhone 12 mini language

Success! You have just updated your iPhone language!

CHAPTER EIGHT

GET STARTED AND START WITH FAMILY SHARING ON

The family organizer is the person who needs to establish a family partnership first. As a family organizer, you are the one who receives purchase requests, and more importantly, you agree to pay for all the purchases made by everyone in the family group, adult or child.

- Open the Settings app
- Tap the Apple ID banner above.
- Tap the Family Sharing Setup.
- Tap Start.
- Tap Continue. You can attach a photo in advance if you want, but it is not required.
- Tap Continue to share purchases.
- Tap Next to confirm your form of payment.
- Tap Share your location to share it with family or tap Not now.
- Tap Add Family Member and add the person you want to add.

Start typing there.

- Input your credit card security code details when ask

hat's it! Just add more friends until everyone in your amily joins (up to 6 people). They will receive an email as vell as a push notification on their devices asking them to iccept your order. If so, all purchases made from that noment will be credited to the family organizer account. And they have instant access to all the others in the group purchases.

HOW TO ACCEPT A FAMILY SHARING INVITATION

- Start settings from the home screen.
- Tap the Apple ID banner above.
- Tap Orders. Should be number 1 next to it (unless you have other orders to wait).
- Tap Accept

Alternatively, you can select a different Apple ID by clicking "on (your name) or using a different ID?"

HOW TO DESIGNATE YOURSELF AS A PARENT OR GUARDIAN

Remember that in order to reach someone as a parent or guardian, you must be the family organizer, that is, the person who builds the family sharing group.

- Open the Settings app
- Tap the Apple ID banner above.
- Tap Family Sharing.
- Tap the person you want to assign as a parent or guardian.
- Tap the switch next to the parent / guardian to turn it on (green is on).

That's it. The same person will now receive purchase requests from all the children in your family sharing group. This means that if one person is busy and cannot approve a request, the other parent can. You still only need one person to receive a request, not both.

CHAPTER NINE

REMINDER

HOW TO CREATE A NEW REMINDER

Start with memories

Create a reminder, add useful details and then mark it as complete when you have done so.

How to create reminder

- Open the Reminders app.
- Tap + New Reminder and enter your reminder.
- Tap Done..

RECEIVE A REMINDER WHEN SENDING MESSAGES TO SOMEONE

Open if you have messages when you want to be notified when you are chatting with a certain person in the messages.

- Open When sending message, tap Select person and then click on a name in your contacts.

The next time you talk to this person, a reminder message will appear.

CHAPTER TEN

CUSTOMIZE XBOX ONE CONTROLLER WITH IPHONE

- Open the settings app.
- Click Bluetooth. Bluetooth may already be there, but if not, the Bluetooth at the top of the next page will turn green.

While the Bluetooth menu is still open, lift your Xbox One controller and make sure it is charged. Make it happen by clicking the Xbox logo button.

- Press and hold the wireless sign-in button on the back of your Xbox One controller for a few seconds. The light on the Xbox button should start flashing quickly (if your Xbox One controller is not yet connected from another device, you can usually skip this step. A long press on the Xbox button will be enough to put it in pairing mode.)

On your iPhone 12 mini you should see the "Xbox Wireless Controller" among other devices in the Bluetooth menu. Click on it.

The light on your Xbox button should stop flashing immediately and stay on.

It have been connected.

PAIR A DUALSHOCK 4 COTROLLER WITH IPHONE 12 MINI

- Open the settings app.
- Click Bluetooth. Bluetooth may already be there, but if not, the Bluetooth at the top of the next page will turn green.

While the Bluetooth menu is still open, lift the DualShock 4 controller and make sure it is charged.

- press and hold the PlayStation button at ones and the share button for a few seconds. The light on the back of your DualShock 4 should start flashing again..

The light on the back of your DualShock 4 should immediately change to a red-pink color. Your DualShock 4 is now optimized.

CHAPTER ELEVEN

HOW TO USE PICTURE-IN-PICTURE MODE

- Open a compatible video application, such as the Apple TV application
- Search for your video content
- Press the power button
- In the upper right corner tap on the image icon in the image

You can move the video box up and down on the screen to find a better viewing position when you are doing other things.

If you find that you want to look back to your full video screen, just click on the image icon in the image in the video - this time it will move to the top left corner.

Note to YouTube: The YouTube app restricts image-by-image to premium subscribers. Users could - for one day - see the PiP content on the YouTube site as a solution, but apparently this gap was closed. Interestingly, the videos embedded in third-party sites still match the feature.

CHAPTER TWELVE

CHANGE WALLPAPER

First, let's learn how to change your iPhone wallpapers using Apple's stock library. In addition, some wallpapers change when you use dark mode.

- Open the settings app
- Scroll down and tap Wallpaper.
- Tap Select New Wallpaper.
- Choose the wallpaper you want to.

❏ Dynamic: This is an image from Apple's photo library with effects that fade and respond to the movement of your device.

❏ Still: This is a still image from Apple's photo library.

❏ Live: These wallpapers create a little animation when you tap and hold your finger.

Select an image to enter preview mode.

In preview mode, you can select to turn the perspective zoom on or off. When you release it, you will see your wallpaper move when you tilt your iPhone.

Choose whether you want this wallpaper for the lock screen, the home screen, or both.

SETUP LIVE PHOTOS AS WALLPAPER FOR LOCK SCREEN

- Go to Settings> Wallpaper.

- Tap Select New Wallpaper. Scroll down and tap on live images.

- Select an image. Make sure you have a live image: Enabled.

- Tap the fence. Select Set Lock Screen or Set Both Setting the home screen is not critical because the wallpaper does not really move on the home screen.

ADD A NEW WIDGET TO HOME SCREEN

Add widgets to your home screen

- From the Home screen, touch and hold an apple or an empty area until the apps vibrate.

- Tap the Add Gray button in the upper right corner.

- Select a widget, select from three widget sizes and click Add Widget.

- Tap Done.

You can also add Today's View widgets. From the day view, touch and hold the widget until the quick action menu opens, then click Edit home screen. Drag the widget to the far right of the screen until it appears on the home screen and then tap Done.

EDIT A WIDGET

Modify your widgets

IOS 14 lets you configure your widgets.

Hold the widget and the Quick Actions menu will open then,

- Tap Edit Widget Edit Widget Icon.

Make the changes and click outside the widget to exit.

You can also move your widgets to place your favorites where they are easier to find. Just touch and hold the widget until it giggles and then move the widget to the screen.

ADD WIDGET TO THE TODAY VIEW

- Add widgets to day view
- Touch and hold the widget or empty area in the day view until the apps giggle.
- Tap the Add Gray Plus Icon icon in the top right corner.

- Scroll down to select a widget, then select from three widget sizes.
- Tap Add widget and click Done.

CREATE A SMART STACK

A smart cartridge automatically rotates widgets to display relevant information throughout the day.

- Touch and hold the area on your home screen or day view until the apps giggle.
- Tap the Add Gray Plus Icon icon in the top right corner.
- Scroll down and tap Smart Stack.
- Tap Add widget.

A stack of widgets is displayed on the iPhone

CREATE YOUR OWN STACK OF WIDGETS

- Touch and hold the app or an empty area on the home screen or day view until the apps shake.
- Drag a widget onto another widget.
- Tap Done.

CHANGE WIDGET STACK

- Touch and hold the widget stack.

- Tap to change stack. From here you can reorder the widgets in the stack by dragging the web icon three gray lines. Or millions of users share a widget that is left to delete.

- Tap the gray icon x to remove it when done.

CHAPTER THIRTEEN

SETUP CARPLAY

Connect your iPhone with CarPlay

Set up CarPlay by connecting your iPhone and vehicle to your USB port or wireless feature.

- Make sure Siri is enable on your iPhone
- If Siri is not enabled on your iPhone, go to Settings> Pots and Search, then enable one of the following:
- Press the side button for the pots (on iPhone with Face ID)

CONNECCT WITH USB

Connect your iPhone to your vehicle's USB port using an Apple-approved USB Lightning Cable.

You can mark the USB port with the CarPlay logo or a picture of a smartphone.

CONNECTION WITHOUT CABLE OR WIRELESSLY

- Hold the voice command button
- Your vehicle must be in wireless or Bluetooth pairing mode.

- Go to Settings> General> CarPlay> Cars Available on your iPhone.
- Choose your vehicle.

Note: Some vehicles that support wireless CarPlay allow you to easily connect using your vehicle's iPhone and USB port using a USB lightning cable. If supported after playing CarPlay with USB, you will be asked if you want to adapt Wireless CarPlay for future use. If you agree, the next time you drive, the iPhone will automatically connect to CarPlay.

On some car models, CarPlay Home appears automatically when you connect the iPhone.

If CarPlay Home does not appear, select the CarPlay logo on your vehicle view.

CHAPTER FOURTEEN

TURN VOICE CONTROL

If you are using voice control for the first time, you must configure it by following these steps:

- Start settings from the home screen.

- Tap Accessibility.

- Tap Voice Control.

- Continue tapping "Welcome to Voice Control".

- Tap Next on "What can I say?" screen.

- Set voice control: Tap Continue and then Continue.

TURN ON VOICE CONTROL

If you used voice control before turning it on or off, follow these steps:

- Start settings from the home screen.

- Tap Accessibility.

- Tap Voice Control.

- Tap the on / off control switch. If green is shown, then it has been activated.

CHAPTER FIVTEEN

ADD ANOTHER RINGTONE TO A CONTACT

- Open the Contacts app.
- Select a contact, tap Edit, tap a ringtone and then select a ringtone.
- Turn the ringtone on or off

Turn the ring / silent switch to put the iPhone in ringing mode or silent mode. Clock alarms still ring when the iPhone is in silent mode.

To mute a call, do not interrupt.

HOW TO CHOOSE MESSAGE TONE

Change the default SMS / Text tone

To change the sound you hear for any approaching words:

- Open settings
- Tap a sound
- Tap Text tone
- Select a new sound (Preview of the sound being played as you type)

That's all there's to it. All new text messages activate the new tone when they arrive.

CHANGE THE SMS / TEXT TONE OF A SINGLE CONTACT

- Launch the Contacts app (or the Phone app and select the Contacts tab)
- Tap on their name of the contact you want personalize to open their contact page
- Tap for change
- Tap a tone of text
- Select a new sound

HOW TO SET/CHANGE LANGUAGE

You can change the language setting on iPhone, iPad or iPod touch if it is wrong or if you accidentally changed the language to one that you did not understand.

- Open settings
- Tap General
- On the next screen, tap General.
- Select Language & Region
- Find Language & Region and tap on it.
- Tap Device Language
- Next, tap"Device Language".
- Choose your language
- Select your language from the list.

- Confirm your selection

Your device will automatically update the language.

HOW TO SET/CHANGE DATE AND TIME

- Settings> General> Date & Time.
- Turn off the device automatically.

You can now change the time zone or the date and time:

- Tap the area zone and enter a city with the time zone you need. Use the time zone map at timeanddate.com to find a city with a time zone that meets your needs.)

Or type the date to change the date and time.

CHAPTER SIXTEEN

MESSAGE APP

SETUP IMESSAGE

How to turn iMessages on or off for iPhone or iPad

If you set up your iPhone with iCloud, chances are iMessage was activated using it. If not, or if you ever need to restart it, it's easy to do!

- Start settings from the home screen.
- Tap Messages.
- You can click on the iMessage on / off switch.

When it turn green know it's activated.

SET UP YOUR DEVICE FOR MMS

Set up your mobile phone to MMS

You can send and receive MMS as soon as you log in to your SIM. If this is not the case then maybe your phone can be set up manually for MMS.

- Tap Settings.
- Tap Messages.
- Tap the slider next to "MMS" to turn on the feature.

PIN AND UNPIN MESSAGE

How to Pair Messaging Calls on iPhone with iOS 14

- Go to the messaging app.

- Tap "Edit". In the upper right corner,

- Tap "Edit" in the upper right corner of the messaging app.

- Tap "Edit" in the upper right corner of the messaging app.

- Click "Edit Pins".

- "Edit Pins" from the drop menu..

- Snap messages at the top of the app by tapping the yellow pin icon next to the call.

- Tap the yellow pin icon to catch a call.

- Tap the yellow pin icon to catch a call.

- When done, click "done".

Alternatively, you can pin a call to the top of the app by right-clicking on a call and then tapping "Snap".

You can also press and hold a call and select "Snap" from the drop-down menu.

You can also press and hold a call and select "Snap" from the drop-down menu.

DELETE A MESSAGE

- From the Home screen, tap Messages.
- Tap the message you want want.
- Tap more ...
- Tap the trash icon.
- Tap Delete message.

CHAPTER SEVENTEEN

SETUP MAIL ACCOUNT

If you use an email provider like iCloud, Google or Yahoo, Mail can set up your email account automatically only with your email address and password.

- Go to Settings> Mail, then click Accounts.
- Tap Add account
- Enter your email address and password.
- Tap Next and you will wait to confirm for account.

Select information from your e-mail account, such as contacts or calendars.

- Tap Save.

If you do not see your email provider, tap others to manually add your account.

The iPhone shows how to add a mail account manually

SET UP YOUR EMAIL ACCOUNT MANUALLY

If you do not know them, you can search for them or contact your email provider. Then follow these steps:

- Go to Settings> Mail, then click Accounts.

- Tap Add Account, tap Another, then tap Add Mail Account.

- You need to input your email address, password name, and also the description for your account.

- Tap Next. Mail tries to find your email settings and complete your account creation. When Mail finds your email settings, tap Done to complete your account creation.

DELETE EMAIL ACCOUNT

If you have problems sending and receiving e-mails, you can delete the e-mail account and then create it again.

- Find "Accounts"
- Click on a position.
- Click Mail.
- Click Account.
- Enter the required email account.
- Click Delete Account.
- Click Delete from My iPhone.
- Return to the home screen

RECOVER DELETE EMAILS

Launch the mail app. On the home screen of your iPhone, tap the white envelope icon with the blue background. The mail application interface is loaded on the screen.

Shake your phone. If you accidentally delete an email, just tap your iPhone by hand. A set of pop-ups: "Undo trash?" And "cancel".

Restore Email. Tap "Cancel" and the deleted email will be restored to your inbox.

Note that this only works for deleted emails. If you leave the mail app, you will not be able to retrieve mail.

CHAPTER EIGHTEEN

TAKE A SCREENSHOT ONYOUR DEVICE WITH FACE ID

- Touch and hold the volume up button, and side button.

- Release both buttons quickly.

After taking a screenshot, a thumbnail will temporarily appear in the far left corner of the screen. Tap the thumbnail to open it or left click to release it.

• HOW TO TAKE A SCREENSHOT OF IPHONE MODELS WITH A TOUCH ID AND SIDE BUTTON

- Touch and hold the home button and the side button.
- Release both buttons quickly.

After taking a screenshot, a thumbnail will temporarily appear in the far left corner of the screen. Tap the thumbnail to open it or left click to release it.

CHAPTER NINTEEN

SET UP THE HEADPHONE LEVEL CHECKER

- Open the settings app.

- Click on Control Center.

- Scroll down and press the green plus (+) button next to Audio.

HOW TO USE A HEADPHONE LEVEL TESTER IN IOS 14

The next time you hear something on your iOS device using connected headphones, follow these steps.

- Start control center

n iPad with the Home button, double-click the Home button; On iPhone 8 and above, swipe up from the bottom of the screen; And on iPad Pro 2018 or iPhone X or later, ap from the top right corner of the screen.

- Check the hearing

Aids in the control center. If it has a green mark, listen to a healthy volume level. If what you are listening to is above 80 decibels, the measurement icon will display a

yellow exclamation mark, warning you that the volume is
too high.

For a more detailed picture of the current decibel level,
press the listen button.

USE APPLE'S LIVE LIST FEATURE WITH AIRPODS

The real-time headphone-level feature works well with
most headphones, but keep in mind that Apple says the
measurement is more accurate with AirPods and other
Apple-approved headphones.

CHAPTER TWENTY

SET A SLEEP SCHEDULE ON IPHONE

- Open the Health app.

- Tap the Browse tab in the lower right corner of the screen.

- Scroll down and select Sleep.

- Tap on the sleep schedule under "Your Schedule".

- When the sleep program is off, press the button to switch to the green ON mode.

- Under "Full schedule", type your first schedule.

- Tap on one of the blue circles in the "Active Days" section to turn off the sleep panel any day of the week.

- Using your finger, pull the edge of the sleeping pad to extend it around the clock graph. It defines your sleep progress as well as your bedtime and wake time.

- Scroll down to find out your alarm options. Use the switch next to the wake-up alarm to turn the alarm on / off. Once you have activated the alarm, you can select the type of vibration and sound you want to hear using Sounds & Haptics, adjust the volume using the slider and enable snooze using the snooze switch.

- Tap Add in the top right corner when done.
- To add an additional schedule for different days (for example, on weekends), type a schedule for other days and customize your options as described in the previous steps.

Note that if this is the first time you are setting a sleep schedule after opening the health app and navigating to the sleep section, you will need to tap "Start work" and set a sleep destination before you can set the sleep and adjust the schedule.

CHAPTER TWENTY ONE

MANAGE APPLICATIONS AND DATA

INSTALL APPS FROM THE APP STORE

Once you have searched for the app you are looking for, it is time to download and install it.

- Tap the app or game you want to buy or download for free.
- Tap Get when it's free, or the price of the app when it's paid.
- Move your finger on the Home Button to activate a Touch ID or double-click the Face ID side button.

HOW TO DELETE APPS

Similar to switching to "past mode" on devices with a three-dimensional touch in the past, the key is to place your finger on an app (no need to press down hard) for a second.

- Look for the app you don't need or would like to uninstall on the device home screen.
- Press and hold the app
- Tap Delete app when menu options appear.

HOW TO DELETE MULTIPLE APPS

Missing the good old days of "juggling mode" on your home screen? It's still there.

Select an app on your home screen (no matter which one you choose).

- Press and hold the app icon for two seconds.
- Tap the X in the top right corner of any app icon you want to remove.
- Tap Finish in the top right corner of your iPhone (or click the Home button on iPhones with one) when done.

CHAPTER TWENTY TWO

LOCATION SERVICES

ENABLE LOCATION SERVICES

How to activate location on iPhone 12

Tasks

Activating location is very useful and essential for using maps in various apps like Uber.

We'll show you how to manage and configure location settings on your iPhone 12 so you can enjoy the benefits of location services.

- Go to Home screen settings.
- Select Privacy.
- Click Location Services and turn on the feature.

Now the applications that need to know your location will send you an alert requesting your access permission

- Never
- Ask next time
- While using the app
- All the time

Congratulations, you have now activated location on your iPhone 12.

CHAPTER TWENTY THREE

HOW TO CREATE A NEW APPLE ID

- Launch the settings app.
- Tap Connect on your iPhone at the top of the screen.
- Apple ID shows the steps to enable the settings, then click Sign In
- Tap Do not have an Apple ID or have you forgotten it?
- Click on Create Apple ID.

Apple ID on iPhone Displays the steps Tap Do not Apple ID then tap Create Apple Apple

- Enter date of birth.
- Tap Next.
- Enter your first and last name.
- Tap Next.
- Input your email address or get a new iCloud email address.

Apple ID on iPhone Displays the steps for entering a birthday for the new Apple ID on iPhone

- Enter your email address.
- Create a password.

- Confirm the password.

- Select a security question.

- Type and answer.

- Repeat two more times.

- Enter security questions for a new Apple ID on iPhone

- Agree to the terms.

- Tap Merge.

- Tap Done to confirm.

SETUP GOOGLE MAIL

How to access Google mail, calendar and contacts on iPhone

- Open settings.

- Scroll down and tap Mail.

- Tap Accounts.

- Select Add Account.

- Tap Google.

- Tap Continue when prompted to confirm that Google.com allows you to sign in to your iPhone or iPad.

- Enter your Google Account login information.

Make sure the mail switches, contacts, and calendars in "on" or "off" locations hang where you want them.

- Tap Save.

CHAPTER TWENTY FOUR

APPLE PAY

ADD A CREDIT CARD OR DEBIT CARD

In the wallet, tap the Add Card button.

Do one of the following:

- Add a new card or your previous one.
- Tap Next and enter the CVV number of each card.

Alternatively, you can attach your card from the bank app or card issuer.

The card changer will determine if your card is eligible for Apple Pay, and may ask you for more information to complete the verification process.

The first card you add to your wallet will be the default payment card. To set another card by default, move it to the front of the stack.

Wallet selects your default card.

Touch and hold the card and then pull it to the front of the stack.

To place another card, touch and hold it and then drag it to a new location.

SEND PAYMENT IN MESSAGES

How do I send payments using Apple Pay Cash

Sending money to friends and family in messages is strangely similar to sending a sticker.

- Open the messages app
- Tap a conversation with the person you want to send money to or start a new iMessage conversation.
- Click on the Apple Pay button.
- Send payments and notifications, show how to open notifications, tap a call and click the Apple Pay button
- Press the - or + buttons to select an amount.
- Tap Show keyboard if you want to enter a specific amount.

Enter your specific amount.

Send payments and notifications, and press the - or + button, then click Show Keyboard and enter your amount

- Tap Pay.

- Press the Submit button (looks like an arrow in a black circle).

Confirm payment by an Apple Pay connected bank card.

Send payments and messages, tap on payment and then tap on send, which is the payment